HTML Copy, CSS Paste: The Only Guide You'll Ever Need

FOR ABSOLUTE BEGINNERS
WITH PROJECTS

MAJELLA RAJAN

II

Copyright © 2024 A. N. Other. All rights reserved. No part of this book may be used or reproduced without the written consent of the copyright owner

IBSN: 9798333854223

Written, Edited, Published By Majella Rajan.

visit her website majellarajan.com

III

Table of Contents

Introduction — VI
What is coding? — 1
What to use it for? — 1
How to go further in learning? — 2

Set up to Code — 3
Visual Studio Code — 3
Replit — 5

Level 1 — 8

HTML — 9

Intro to HTML — 9
- Understanding Markup Language — 9
- What HTML Does — 9
- HTML vs CSS — 10
- Role of HTML in web development — 10
- Basic HTML doc — 11

HTML tags — 13
- Nesting tags — 13

Basic Tags to Know — 13
HTML Attributes — 15
- Anchor Tag and HREF Attribute — 15

Level 2   19

CSS   20

Intro to CSS   20
Using Style   20
Using Hexadecimal Color Codes   20
Adding CSS to the page   20
Body Styles   23
Changing fonts   24
Classes and IDs   26
Border   28
Margin and Padding   30
Side by Side Divs   33

Level 3   35

Test your knowledge   36

Quiz 1 - (HTML)   36
Quiz 2 - (CSS)   38
Answer Key   40

Portfolio   43

What is a digital portfolio   43

- target audience 44
- unique value proposition 45
- setting metrics for success 46

Building your portfolio sections 47
Responsive Design 48

Level 4 — 51

Appendix — 52

Hexadecimal Color Codes Explained 52
Counting in Hexadecimal 52
Additive Color Theory 53
Applying Color Codes in Design 53

Level 5 — 55

Javascript — 56

What is Javascript 56
Why is JavaScript Essential for Web Development? 56
Setting Up JavaScript in a Web Page 56
Quick Run Through of Javascript 56

Level 6 — 63

Future Learning 64

Website Ideas 64
Domains to Publish 66
Future Books 70
 Way2Eazy 72

Level 7 72

Notes 73

Introduction

What is Coding?

Coding is like giving directions to a computer. Just as you might tell a friend how to get from point A to point B, coding involves writing step-by-step instructions for a computer to perform a task. These instructions, written in a specific programming language, are called **code**. There are multiple languages in technology! In the context of **web development**, **HTML** (HyperText Markup Language) and **CSS** (Cascading Style Sheets) are fundamental languages that allow developers to create and style web pages. HTML forms the structure of a webpage, defining its content like text, images, and links. CSS, on the other hand, determines how these elements are presented, specifying aspects such as colors, layouts, and fonts.

What to use it for?

Coding with HTML and CSS allows you to build websites and web applications. Here are some common uses:

- Building Websites: Create personal blogs, business pages, portfolios, and more.
- Enhancing User Experience: Use CSS to design intuitive layouts, improve readability, and create visually engaging content.
- Responsive Design: Ensure your websites look great on all devices, from desktops to smartphones, using responsive design principles.

- Integration: Combine HTML and CSS with other languages like JavaScript for dynamic functionality and interaction.
- Career Opportunities: Web development skills are in high demand across industries, offering opportunities for freelance work, full-time employment, and entrepreneurial ventures.

How to go further in learning after this book?

This book is only the beginners guide to making webpages. To go even deeper into coding and Java, go to way2eazy.org (a non-profit website dedicated to teaching kids to code) for coding activities and ask questions in the forum. Remember learning coding is essentialy like learning any new skill – it takes practice and patience so have FUN!

Set up your Coding Place

How to use Visual Studio Code?

Step 1: Install Visual Studio Code (if not already installed)
If you haven't already installed Visual Studio Code on your computer, you can download it from the official website: Visual Studio Code Download.

Step 2: Open Visual Studio Code
- Launch Visual Studio Code by clicking on its icon in the Applications folder or by searching for it using Spotlight.

Step 3: Create a New HTML File
- Open a New Window: If Visual Studio Code opens a previous project, close it to start fresh.

- Create a New File:
    - Click on File in the top menu.
    - Select New File from the dropdown menu.
    - Alternatively, you can use the shortcut Cmd + N to create a new file.
- Save the File:
    - After creating a new file, immediately save it by clicking on File > Save or using the shortcut Cmd + S.
    - Choose a location on your Mac where you want to save the file.
    - Name your file with an .html extension, for example, index.html.

Step 4: View your Webpage

After writing your HTML code, you can preview your webpage in a browser to see how it looks.

- Save the HTML File: Make sure to save any changes (Cmd + S).
- Open the File in a Browser:
- Right-click on the HTML file (index.html in this case) in Visual Studio Code.
- Select Reveal in Finder to locate the file in Finder.
- Double-click on the file to open it in your default web browser (Safari, Chrome, Firefox, etc.).

How to use Replit?

What is Replit?

Replit is an online IDE (Integrated Development Environment) that supports a variety of programming languages and frameworks. It offers features like live previews, collaborative coding, and cloud-based storage, making it an excellent tool for both beginners and experienced developers.

Setting Up Your Replit Account
1. Sign Up or Log In:
    - Go to Replit's website.
    - If you don't have an account, click on "Sign Up" and choose a sign-up method (email, Google, or GitHub). If you already have an account, click "Log In" and enter your credentials.
2. Creating a New Repl:
    - Once logged in, click on the "+ Create" button on your dashboard.
    - Choose "HTML, CSS, JS" from the list of templates. This template is pre-configured for web development and will create a project with an index.html, style.css, and script.js file.
3. Naming Your Repl:
    - Enter a name for your project in the "Title" field. This name will be used for the project and will help you keep your work organized.
    - Click "Create Repl" to initialize your project.

Exploring the Replit Interface
1. Editor Pane:
    - On the left side of the screen, you'll see the file explorer where you can access and manage your

HTML, CSS, and JavaScript files. You can add new files or folders here as needed.
- The central area is the code editor where you write and edit your code. Replit provides syntax highlighting and code suggestions to make your coding experience smoother.

1. Preview Pane:
   - On the right side of the screen, you'll find the preview pane. This is where you can see the live output of your HTML and CSS code. Replit automatically refreshes this pane as you save changes to your code.
2. Console:
   - Below the preview pane, the console shows any errors or logs related to your code. It's useful for debugging and seeing the results of your JavaScript code.

Viewing Changes:
- As you make changes to your HTML or CSS files, Replit automatically updates the preview pane. This allows you to see the results of your code in real-time.

Debugging:
- If you encounter issues, check the console for error messages. Common issues might include syntax errors in your HTML or CSS, or issues with linking your CSS file.

To collaborate:
- Replit allows you to collaborate on projects in real-time. To invite collaborators, click on the "Share" button in the top-right corner of the editor.
- You can share the project via a link or invite specific users by email.

Sharing Your Project:
If you want to share your project with others, you can use the "Share" button to get a shareable link. This link can be shared with anyone who you want to view or interact with your project.

MORE FEATURES:

Version Control:
Replit includes version control features that allow you to track changes to your code. You can use the version history to revert to previous versions of your project if needed.

Extensions and Packages:
Replit supports various extensions and packages that you can integrate into your project. Explore the "Packages" tab to add additional tools or libraries.

Deployment:
For advanced users, Replit offers deployment options to publish your project online. This feature is useful if you want to make your project accessible to a wider audience.

LEVEL 1!

Intro to HTML

So what is HTML? HTML stands for HyperText Markup Language, but what does that mean for you? Essentially, HTML is a language designed to structure and organize content on web pages. It acts like a set of instructions that tells a web browser how to display text, images, links, and other media.

Understanding Markup Language

HTML is often referred to as a "markup language." This term might sound technical, but it's quite straightforward. Imagine you have a document (your webpage) and you want to highlight certain parts, like making a heading or emphasizing a word. HTML provides specific tags (like <h1>, <p>, <em>) that you wrap around your content to give it meaning. These tags are like signposts that tell the browser, "Hey, this part is a heading," or "This text should be emphasized."

What HTML Does

In HTML, you're specifying the structure and semantics of your content. Structure means organizing your content into paragraphs, lists, headings, and sections. Semantics refers to the meaning behind your content—for example, distinguishing between a main heading (<h1>) and a subheading (<h2>).

HTML vs. CSS

Moving along, it's crucial to grasp the distinction between HTML and CSS. HTML tells the browser what each piece of content is (like a title or paragraph), while CSS (Cascading Style Sheets) determines how those elements should look. For instance, if you want a heading to appear larger and bold, you specify that with CSS. HTML remains focused on defining the content itself, leaving the presentation details to CSS.

The Role of HTML in Web Development

HTML forms the backbone of every webpage. It provides the essential structure and semantics that browsers use to render content. Without HTML, web pages would be chaotic and difficult to navigate. By learning HTML, you gain the foundational skills needed to create clear, organized, and accessible websites. As we progress, you'll see how HTML tags work in practice and how to use them effectively to build web pages. Remember, HTML is about structuring content—defining what each piece of information is. CSS, which we'll cover later, focuses on styling and presentation.

Basic HTML Doc

Lets start by creating a basic HTML document.

```html
<!DOCTYPE html>
<html>
<head>
    <title>My First Page</title>
</head>
<body>
    <h1>Hello World!</h1>
    <p>This is a paragraph of plain text.</p>
</body>
</html>
```

1. **<!DOCTYPE html>:**

This declaration (DOCTYPE) defines the document type and version of HTML being used, which in this case is HTML5 (html). It informs the web browser how to interpret the rest of the document's content.

2. **<html>:**

The <html> tag serves as the root element of the HTML document. It encapsulates all the content that makes up the web page.

3. **<head>:**

Inside the <html> element, the <head> tag contains metadata about the HTML document. Metadata includes information such as the document's title (<title>), character set declarations, links to external stylesheets or scripts, and more.

4. **<title>:**

The <title> tag, placed within the <head> section, defines the title of the web page. This title appears in the browser's title bar or tab, providing users with a brief description of the page's content.

5.<body>:
Within the <html> element, the <body> tag encloses all the visible content of the web page that users interact with. This includes text, images, links, headings (<h1>, <h2>, etc.), paragraphs (<p>), lists (<ul>, <ol>, <li>), forms (<form>, <input>, <button>), and more.

6.<h1> and <p>:
These are content tags used within the <body> section to structure and present content to users.

7.<h1>:
Defines a level 1 heading, which is typically used as the main heading of the page. It is the largest and most prominent heading size.

8.<p>:
Represents a paragraph of text. It is used to structure and organize blocks of text on the page, providing readability and structure to the content.

HTML Tags

If you've ever seen HTML before, you know there are a lot of things that go in between < and > signs. These things are called tags. There are two types of tags in HTML, but we're going to just worry about one to begin with. The first type of tag is the opening and closing tag. Here is an example:

<em>cool</> explosion

There are a couple of things to note about this example. Let's not worry about what <em> means, and just focus on the basic syntax. First, notice how there is a forward slash in the second </em> tag. That indicates that it is a closing tag. The first <em> tag is an opening tag. Everything in between the opening and closing tags is affected by the tag. Thus, in this example, the word "cool" will be affected by the <em> tags, but the word "cool" will not be affected (it is outside the tags). Pretty simple so far, right?

Nesting Tags

You can place these tags inside of each other. This is called nesting tags in programmer speak. For example:

<em>cool <strong>explosion</strong></em>

Here, the word "cool" is affected by only the <em> tag, but the word "explosion" is affected by both the <em> and <strong> tags.

Basic Tags to know

Tags become more enjoyable once you have a couple to experiment with. Here are some basic tags that every novice HTML coder should familiarize themselves with. These are all opening and closing tags, which means they affect the text they enclose. We'll delve into the second type of tag soon.

- **em:** Stands for emphasis and is used to emphasize text. By default, this renders as italic.
- **strong:** Used for text that is strongly important. By default, this renders as bold.
- **h1:** Stands for header 1 and is the largest type of header, typically used for page titles. There are also tags h2 through h6, which get progressively smaller and are used for subheaders or subtitles. By default, h1 renders as bold, large text on its own line.
- **p**: Stands for paragraph and should be used to enclose paragraphs of text. By default, this adds space before and after the paragraph, simulating the effect of pressing enter twice on your keyboard.
- **ol and ul:** These are ordered list and unordered list tags, used for numbered and bulleted lists, respectively. Each item in the list should be within an li (list item) tag.
- **div:** Stands for division, representing a section of the page. This versatile tag is used to organize more complex HTML into sections. Its use becomes more apparent in the CSS section.

These tags form the building blocks of HTML, enabling you to structure and organize content effectively on web pages. As you practice using these tags, you'll gain a solid foundation for creating clear and well-structured web documents.

HTML Attributes

In HTML, tags can have attributes that provide additional information or modify the behavior of the element. Let's explore the anchor (<a>) tag as an example, which is used for creating links in web pages. Attributes are specified within the opening tag and always follow the syntax ATTRIBUTE="VALUE", with the value enclosed in quotes.

Anchor Tag and HREF Attribute

The anchor tag (<a>) is primarily used to create hyperlinks. It has an attribute called href, short for "hypertext reference," which specifies the URL (web address) of the page that the link points to. Here's an example:

In this example:
- <a>: This is the anchor tag.
- **href="http://way2eazy.com":** This attribute tells the browser to link to the webpage located at http://way2eazy.com.
- Click Here: This is the visible text or content of the link that users will see on the webpage.

How it Works
When a user clicks on the link rendered by the anchor tag, the browser navigates to the URL specified in the href attribute. This allows users to easily navigate between different web pages or websites.

Using Relative Paths
Instead of specifying a full URL, you can use relative paths for the href attribute. Relative paths are relative to the location of the current HTML file.

Tags that Stand-alone

In HTML, tags are categorized into two types: opening and closing tags, and stand-alone tags. Opening and closing tags typically enclose content to apply formatting or structure. In contrast, stand-alone tags are self-contained and do not require enclosing content. Let's explore a couple of essential stand-alone tags: <br> and <img>.

 Tag

The <br> tag is one of the simplest stand-alone tags in HTML. It stands for "line break" and is used to insert a line break within text content, similar to pressing Enter on your keyboard. Here's an example:

**This is the first line.
**
This is the second line.

In this example, <br> creates a line break after "first line," causing "second line" to appear on a new line.

<img> Tag

The <img> tag is used to embed images in an HTML document. It is a stand-alone tag because it does not have a closing tag and is self-contained. The <img> tag requires the src attribute, which specifies the URL (web address) of the image file. Optionally, it can also include width and height attributes to define the dimensions of the displayed image in pixels. Here's an example:

`<img src="https://way2eazy/assets/html_logo.png" width="100" height="100">`

What will the code above look like? Try it yourself!

1. Open your index.html file from before.
2. Add the img code above somewhere in the file, and save it.
3. Open the file in your web browser (or refresh the page if you already have it open), and voila!

Now, try saving the image to your computer and loading it from your computer instead:

1. Right-click the image and save it as html_logo.png. Save it in the same folder as your index.html file.
2. Change your img tag to the following: <img width="100" height="100" src="html_logo.png">
3. Now refresh the page in your web browser and the image should still show up! Except now it's using the image file on your computer.

Now you know how to save images from the internet to put them in your website.

HTML Structure

When creating web pages with HTML, it's essential to follow a structured format that begins with a declaration and organizes content within <html>, <head>, and <body> tags. Let's go deeper into each component to gain a comprehensive understanding.

Document Type Declaration (<!DOCTYPE html>)

Every HTML document starts with a document type declaration. This line informs the web browser which version of HTML the document adheres to. In modern web development, <!DOCTYPE html> is used to specify that the document conforms to HTML5 standards.

17

HTML Root Element (<html>)

The <html> element serves as the root container for all content on the web page. It encapsulates the entire structure of the document and contains two main sections: <head> and <body>.

Head Section (<head>)

Inside the <head> section, you include metadata and other information about the document that isn't directly displayed on the web page itself. Key elements typically found in the <head> section include:

- **<title>:** Sets the title of the web page, which appears in the browser's title bar or tab.
- **Meta tags**: Provide information such as character set (<meta charset="UTF-8">) and viewport settings (<meta name="viewport" content="width=device-width, initial-scale=1.0">).
- **Link tags:** Link to external resources like stylesheets (<link rel="stylesheet" href="styles.css">) or web fonts.

Body Section (<body>)

The <body> section contains the visible content of the web page that users interact with. It includes various HTML elements like headings (<h1> to <h6>), paragraphs (<p>), lists (<ul>, <ol>, <li>), images (<img>), links (<a>), forms (<form>, <input>, <button>), and more.

Congratulations on sticking with me this far! You now know enough basic HTML to move on to the next section: CSS.

LEVEL 2!

Intro to CSS

CSS, or Cascading Style Sheets, is a language used alongside HTML to define the presentation and layout of web pages. While knowing that it cascades styles from one element to another is interesting, its primary function is to dictate how HTML content should appear. While HTML provides the structure and content of a webpage, CSS enhances this by specifying how elements should be styled and displayed. For instance, while HTML might indicate that a piece of text needs emphasis, it's CSS that defines how that emphasis should show—whether it's through bold text, italics, a vibrant color, or a combination of these effects.

Using Style

When using HTML alone, <strong> tags by default make text bold. However, by incorporating CSS (Cascading Style Sheets), we can elevate the visual impact of these tags further. CSS allows us to manipulate various aspects of how HTML elements appear on a webpage, from text color to background color and more.

Applying CSS to <strong> Tags

To apply CSS styles to <strong> tags, we enclose our CSS rules within <style> tags in the <head> section of our HTML document. Here's an example:

```html
<!DOCTYPE html>
<html>
<head>
  <title>Styling Strong Tags</title>
  <style type="text/css">
    strong {
      color: #eeeeee; /* Sets text color to light gray */
      background-color: #000000; /* Sets background color to black */
      padding: 5px; /* Adds padding around the text */
      border-radius: 5px; /* Rounds the corners of the background */
    }
  </style>
</head>
<body>
  <p>Beautiful <strong>constellations</strong></p>
</body>
</html>
```

CSS Declaration: Inside the <style> tags, we target <strong> elements using the selector strong.

Properties and Values:
- color: #eeeeee;: Changes the text color to light gray using a hexadecimal color code.
- background-color: #000000;: Sets the background color of the <strong> tag to black.
- padding: 5px;: Adds padding around the text inside the <strong> tag to create space.

- border-radius: 5px;: Rounds the corners of the background of the <strong> tag, giving it a softer appearance.

Using Hexadecimal Color Codes

Hexadecimal color codes like #eeeeee and #000000 are a standard way to specify colors in web design. Each code represents a specific color in a format that computers can understand. You can use online color pickers to find the hexadecimal code for any color you wish to use in your CSS. We'll go deeper into color codes later.

Adding CSS to the Page

In an HTML document, the <style> tag is placed within the <head> section. Placing <style> tags here ensures that all styling instructions are loaded before the content of the webpage is rendered.

Here's how your HTML document might look with the <style> tag included in the <head> section:

```
<!DOCTYPE html>
<html>
<head>
  <style type="text/css">
    strong {
      color: #eeeeee; /* Sets text color to light gray */
      background-color: #000000; /* Sets background color to black */
    }
  </style>
  <title>Styling Strong Tags</title>
</head>
<body>
  <p>Beautiful <strong>constellations</strong></p>
</body>
</html>
```

Try it!
1. Copy the above code into a new index.html file and open it in your web browser.
2. Use an online color picker (search for "hexadecimal color picker online") to find more color codes, and try changing the color and background color of the text.
3. Try adding a header (<h1> tag) and try changing the color and background color of this with CSS as well. (Hint: the code we have changes the strong tag, so your code will look very similar to that, but with h1 instead of strong.)

Body Styles

As we learned previously, the <body> tag in an HTML document contains all visible content on the webpage. If we want to change aspects that apply to the entire page, such as background color and font color, we can target the <body> tag itself in CSS. To style the entire webpage using CSS, we use the body selector followed by curly braces { } where we define our desired styles. Here's an example:

```
body {
  background-color: #eeeeee;
  color: #ff0000; // red
}
```

In the CSS example above, you'll notice a line with // red. This is a comment in CSS, denoted by two slashes //. Comments are ignored by the browser and are useful for leaving notes within your CSS code to explain what certain styles do or to remind yourself of details like color codes. Try It Yourself!

1. Experiment with Colors:
    - Copy the above HTML code into your file and open it in your web browser.
    - Observe how the background color of the entire webpage changes to light gray and the font color to red as defined in the CSS for the <body> tag.

2. Adjusting Styles:
    - Modify the hexadecimal color codes (#eeeeee and #ff0000) to different values. Use an online color picker to find new colors and update the CSS accordingly.
    - Notice how changing these values alters the overall look and feel of your webpage.

Changing Fonts

In CSS, the font-family property allows you to specify the typeface (font) that you want to use for text on your webpage. Here's how you can apply different fonts to the entire webpage:

Specifying Specific Fonts

You can specify a specific font name enclosed in single quotes for the font-family property. If the font is installed on the visitor's computer, it will be used:

```
body {
 font-family: 'Arial';
}
```

Using Generic Font Families

Alternatively, you can use generic font families that browsers recognize, ensuring consistency across different devices:

```css
body {
  font-family: sans-serif; /* Uses a sans-serif font like Arial */
}
```

The generic font families you can choose from include:
- serif - fonts with serifs (like Times New Roman)
- sans-serif - fonts without serifs (like Arial)
- cursive - fonts that resemble handwriting
- monospace - fonts where each letter occupies the same amount of horizontal space (useful for code)

Changing Font Size

Adjusting the font size is straightforward using the font-size property in CSS. You can specify the size using various units such as pixels (px), points (pt), or other relative units:

```css
body {
  font-size: 16px; /* Sets font size to 16 pixels */
}
```

Try It Yourself!

Adding Fonts to Your Webpage:
- Open your HTML file and add the font-family CSS property to the body tag.
- Experiment by using a font stack from resources like Modern Font Stacks or specify your own preferred fonts.

Adjusting Font Size:
- Modify the font-size property to see how it affects the readability and appearance of text on your webpage.
- Try using different units like pt or percentages (%) to set the font size.

Classes and IDS

When designing a webpage, it's often necessary to style different sections differently. This is where CSS classes and IDs come into play.

IDs:

An ID in HTML is used to uniquely identify a specific element on a webpage. Typically, IDs are used when there is only one instance of an element that requires styling, such as a header or footer.

- Usage: To assign an ID to an element, you use the id attribute in the HTML tag. For example, <div id="header">...</div>.
- Styling: In CSS, IDs are prefixed with a hash (#) followed by the ID name. This selector targets the specific element with that ID.
- Example: If you have a header with ID "header", you can style it using #header { ... }. This might include properties like width and height.

Classes:

Classes in HTML allow you to group multiple elements together to apply the same styling across them. Unlike IDs, classes can be applied to multiple elements on a page.

- Usage: To assign a class to an element, you use the class attribute. For example, <div class="red">...</div>.
- Styling: In CSS, classes are prefixed with a period (.) followed by the class name. This selector applies styles to all elements that have that class.
- Example: If you have elements with class "red", you can style them using .red { ... }. This might include setting a background-color of #ff0000.

Imagine you want to structure your webpage with a header, content, and footer:

```
<body>
  <div id="header">
    <h1>Welcome to my Webpage!</h1>
  </div>
  <div id="content">
    <p>I'm learning HTML and CSS!</p>
  </div>
  <div class="footer">
    <p>Website made with love.</p>
  </div>
</body>
```

- Header: The <div id="header"> contains the main title of your webpage.
- Content: The <div id="content"> holds the main textual information.
- Footer: The <div class="footer"> is used to indicate information at the bottom of the webpage.

Styling Using CSS:

To style these sections differently:
- You can use #header { ... } to style the header uniquely with properties like background-color, height, and width.
- Use #content { ... } to style the content area with specific font styles, margins, or padding.
- Employ .footer { ... } to style the footer area, perhaps setting a different background color or aligning text differently.

Take the opportunity to experiment with different CSS properties for each section. You can adjust colors, fonts, sizes, and layout properties to achieve the desired look and feel of your webpage.

Border

The border property in CSS allows you to add borders around elements. It consists of three main parts that control the appearance of the border:

Border Width (border-width):
- Specifies the width of the border.
- You can define it using values like 1px, 2px, 3px, etc., where px stands for pixels.
- Alternatively, you can use other units such as em or % for relative sizes.

Border Style (border-style):
- Defines the style of the border line.
- Common values include:
  - solid: Creates a solid line border.
  - dashed: Produces a border made up of dashes.
  - dotted: Creates a border made up of dots.
  - double: Creates a double line border.
  - groove, ridge, inset, outset: These create 3D-like effects around the border.

Border Color (border-color):
- Specifies the color of the border.
- You can use color names (like red, blue, green) or hexadecimal color codes (like #ff0000 for red, #00ff00 for green).
- Hexadecimal color codes provide more precise control over the color appearance.

Applying Borders to HTML Elements

When applying borders to elements in your HTML document, you can target specific elements using IDs or classes:

- ID Selector: Use #header { border: ...; } to apply a border to an element with ID "header".
- Class Selector: Use .footer { border: ...; } to apply a border to elements with class "footer".

Example:

```html
<div id="header">
  <h1>Welcome to my Webpage!</h1>
</div>
<div id="content">
  <p>I'm learning HTML and CSS!</p>
</div>
<div class="footer">
  <p>Website made with love.</p>
</div>
```

To add borders to these sections using CSS:

```css
#header {
  border: 2px solid #00ff00; /* Green solid border with 2 pixels width */
}

#content {
  border: 1px dashed #0000ff; /* Blue dashed border with 1 pixel width */
}

.footer {
  border: 3px dotted #ff0000; /* Red dotted border with 3 pixels width */
}
```

Feel free to experiment with different border properties:
- Adjust the border-width to see how thicker or thinner borders affect the appearance.
- Change the border-style to dashed, dotted, double, or one of the 3D effects (groove, ridge, inset, outset) to see different styles.
- Explore various border-color options using hexadecimal color codes to precisely control the border's color.

Margin and Padding

- The CSS margin property defines the space around an element's border.
- It controls the gap between elements or between an element and its parent container.
- Margin values can be specified in pixels (px), ems (em), percentages (%), or other CSS units.
- For example, setting margin: 20px; on an element will create a 20-pixel space around all sides of the element.
- The CSS padding property determines the space between the element's content and its border.
- It expands the size of the element's content area inside the border.
- Padding values can also be defined in pixels, ems, percentages, etc.
- For instance, padding: 20px; adds a 20-pixel space between the content and the border of the element.

```
#header {
  border: 2px solid #00ff00; /* Green solid border with 2 pixels width */
  margin: 20px; /* Adds 20 pixels margin around the header */
}
```

In this example, the margin: 20px; rule adds 20 pixels of space outside the border of the #header element. This means there will be a gap of 20 pixels between the #header and any adjacent elements or the edges of its parent container.

Next, let's add padding to the #header:

#header {
  border: 2px solid #00ff00; /* Green solid border with 2 pixels width */
  padding: 20px; /* Adds 20 pixels padding inside the header */
}

With padding: 20px;, the space between the content (text or other elements inside #header) and the border of #header will be 20 pixels. This effectively increases the internal space within the #header element.

Differences and Usage
- Margin affects the space outside the border of an element and influences its positioning relative to other elements.
- Padding affects the space inside the border of an element, providing room between the content and the border itself.

Default Behavior
It's important to note that some HTML elements, such as <h1> tags, may have default margin or padding values set by the browser's default stylesheet. These defaults can vary between browsers, which might affect how elements appear if custom margin or padding values are applied.

Practical Example

Consider applying both margin and padding to different elements on your webpage to observe their effects. Use different values and units to understand how they impact spacing and layout.

Partial Borders

To apply a border to only one side of an element, you can use specific border properties:

```
#header {
  border-top: 2px solid #00ff00; /* Border only on the top side */
}
```

In this example, border-top specifies a 2-pixel solid green border only on the top side of the #header element.

Similarly, you can use:
- border-bottom for the bottom side,
- border-left for the left side,
- border-right for the right side.

Partial Margin

To apply margin to specific sides of an element:

```
#header {
  margin-bottom: 20px; /* Margin only on the bottom side */
}
```

Here, margin-bottom adds a 20-pixel margin only on the bottom side of the #header element. You can use:
- margin-top for the top side,
- margin-right for the right side,
- margin-left for the left side.

Partial Padding

To apply padding to specific sides of an element:

#header {
  padding-left: 20px; /* Padding only on the left side */
}

With padding-left, you add a 20-pixel padding only to the left side of the #header element. You can use:
- padding-top for the top side,
- padding-right for the right side,
- padding-bottom for the bottom side.

Side by Side Divs

There is just one last thing before we conclude our basic HTML and CSS tutorial. So far, the header, content, and footer of our page are all on top of each other. But what if we want to have two things side by side? For example, what if we wanted to add a sidebar, next to the content, that is beside it?

The strategy we'll do is this:
1. Put the sidebar and content inside a new div.
2. Set some CSS on this new div to tell it, "put the things inside you side-by-side instead of stacked vertically"

So let's look at how to do this. First, we'll put the sidebar and content in their own div, which I'll give an ID of "main" to in order to be able to select it:

Look at the example on the next page

33

```
<body>
  <div id="header">
      <h1>Welcome to my Webpage!</h1>
  </div>
  <div id="main">
  <div id="sidebar">
      <p>Some links could go here.</p>
  </div>
  <div id="content">
      <p>I'm learning HTML and CSS!</p>
  </div>
  </div>
  <div class="footer">
      <p>Website made with love.</p>
  </div>
</body>
```

Now, we need to put some CSS code on the main div that says, "put everything inside of you side-by-side". This is the code that will do this:

```
#main {
   display: flex;
}
```

In short, this enables something called "flexbox" on the div, which is a modern way to arrange layouts in CSS. By default, something with display: flex will display everything in it side-by-side.

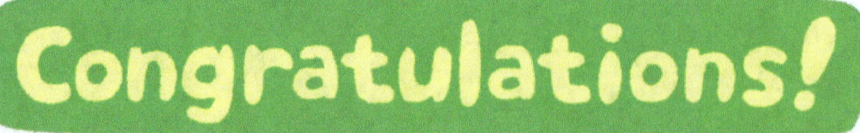

Congratulations on sticking with me this far! You now know enough basic HTML to move on to the next section: Portfolio.

LEVEL 3!

HTML

Quiz 1

Questions
 1. What are HTML tags enclosed by?

a) [and]
b) (and)
c) < and >
d) { and }

 2. What does the <em> tag do to text in HTML?

a) It makes the text bold.
b) It italicizes the text.
c) It underlines the text.
d) It changes the text color.
What distinguishes a closing tag from an opening tag in HTML?

3. What distinguishes a closing tag from an opening tag in HTML?

a) The closing tag has an underscore before the tag name.
b) The closing tag includes a forward slash before the tag name.
c) The closing tag is in uppercase letters.
d) The closing tag has no attributes.

4. How would you create an unordered list in HTML?

a) Using <ol> tags.
b) Using <ul> tags.
c) Using <li> tags alone.
d) Using <dl> tags.

5. What is the purpose of the src attribute in the <img> tag?

a) To define the image file's path.
b) To set the image's width.
c) To specify the image's alt text.
d) To link to an external webpage.

6. Where should the <title> tag be placed in an HTML document?

a) Inside the <body> tag.
b) Inside the <header> tag.
c) Inside the <head> tag.
d) Inside the <footer> tag.

CSS

Quiz 2

1. What does CSS stand for?
   a) Cascading Style Sheets
   b) Creative Style Sheets
   c) Custom Style Sheets
   d) Computer Style Sheets

2. How do you apply CSS to a specific HTML element like <strong>?
   a) Using a class selector
   b) Using an ID selector
   c) Using an element selector
   d) Using an attribute selector

3. What is the purpose of the background-color property in CSS?
   a) To change the text color of an element
   b) To change the color of the borders of an element
   c) To change the background color of an element
   d) To change the font size of an element

4. Where should the <style> tag be placed in an HTML document?

a) Inside the <body> tag
b) Inside the <footer> tag
c) Inside the <head> tag
d) Inside the <div> tag

5. What does the font-family property in CSS do?

a) Sets the color of the text
b) Sets the background color of the text
c) Specifies the font type to be used for the text
d) Sets the size of the font

6. How can you make two div elements appear side-by-side instead of stacked vertically?

a) Using display: block;
b) Using display: inline;
c) Using display: flex;
d) Using display: grid;

Answers and Explanations HTML

1. **Answer: c)** < and >
Explanation: HTML tags are enclosed by angle brackets. For example, <tag> is an opening tag, and </tag> is a closing tag.

2. **Answer: b)** It italicizes the text.
Explanation: The <em> tag is used for emphasizing text, which by default renders as italicized.

3. **Answer: b)** The closing tag includes a forward slash before the tag name.
Explanation: A closing tag has a forward slash (/) before the tag name, such as </tag>, while an opening tag does not.

4. **Answer: b)** Using <ul> tags.
Explanation: The <ul> tag is used to create an unordered (bulleted) list, with each item defined by <li> tags.

5. **Answer: a)** To define the image file's path.
Explanation: The src (source) attribute in the <img> tag specifies the path or URL of the image to be displayed.

6. **Answer: c)** Inside the <head> tag.
Explanation: The <title> tag is placed within the <head> section of the document and determines the text displayed in the browser tab.

What was your score!

/6

Answers and Explanations CSS

1. Answer: a) Cascading Style Sheets
Explanation: CSS stands for Cascading Style Sheets. It is used to control the appearance of web content, including the layout, colors, and fonts of HTML elements.

2. Answer: c) Using an element selector
Explanation: To apply CSS to a specific HTML element, such as <strong>, you use an element selector. This means the styles are applied directly to the element type throughout the page.

3. Answer: c) To change the background color of an element
Explanation: The background-color property is used to set the color that appears behind the content of an element. It changes the background color, making the content stand out more against the background.

4. Answer: c) Inside the <head> tag
Explanation: The <style> tag, which contains CSS rules, should be placed inside the <head> tag of an HTML document. This ensures that styles are applied before the content is rendered.

5. Answer: c) Specifies the font type to be used for the text
Explanation: The font-family property specifies the typeface for text. It determines what font will be used to display the text on the web page.

6. Answer: c) Using display: flex;
Explanation: To arrange two div elements side-by-side, you can use the display: flex; property on their container. This makes the elements align horizontally rather than stacking vertically.

What was your score!

/6

Portfolio

What is a digital portfolio?

Your digital portfolio is more than just a collection of projects; it's a strategic tool to showcase your skills, experience, and personal brand to potential employers, clients, or collaborators. Before diving into the technical aspects of building your portfolio with CSS and HTML, it's essential to clarify its purpose and define your objectives.

Defining Your Goals

Begin by defining the primary goal of your portfolio. Are you aiming to land a job in a specific industry or role? Are you freelancing and seeking clients for web design, graphic design, writing, or another creative field? Are you just trying to build a website? Your goals will shape the content, structure, and overall presentation of your portfolio.

- Career Transition: If you're transitioning to a new career, highlight relevant skills and projects that demonstrate your transferable skills and passion for the new field.

- Freelancing or Contract Work: If you're showcasing your work to attract clients, focus on demonstrating your expertise in solving client problems, delivering results, and showcasing testimonials or case studies.
- Personal Branding: Use your portfolio to establish a personal brand that reflects your unique style, values, and professional identity.

Identifying Your Target Audience

Understanding who will be viewing your portfolio is crucial. Tailor your portfolio content and design to resonate with your target audience, whether it's recruiters, hiring managers, potential clients, or industry peers.

- Recruiters and Hiring Managers: Highlight your professional experience, skills, and achievements relevant to the job you're applying for. Include a resume or CV section and emphasize your career progression and accomplishments.
- Clients: Showcase your portfolio projects that demonstrate your ability to solve their specific problems or achieve their goals. Include client testimonials or case studies to build trust and credibility.
- Industry Peers: Demonstrate thought leadership and expertise in your field by sharing insights, articles, or speaking engagements related to your industry. Engage with professional networks and communities to expand your reach and visibility.

Crafting Your Unique Value Proposition

What sets you apart from others in your field? Your unique value proposition should clearly communicate what makes you the ideal candidate or professional for the

opportunities you seek. Consider the following elements:
- **Skills and Expertise:** Highlight your technical skills, software proficiency, and industry certifications relevant to your target role or industry.
- **Experience and Achievements:** Showcase your past projects, achievements, and measurable results. Use metrics, such as increased revenue, improved efficiency, or client satisfaction scores, to quantify your impact.
- **Passion and Personality:** Infuse your portfolio with your passion for your work and showcase your personality through your writing style, project descriptions, and visual design choices.
- **Professional Goals:** Articulate your career goals and aspirations. Whether you're aiming for leadership roles, entrepreneurial ventures, or industry recognition, align your portfolio content to support your long-term career objectives.

Conducting Competitor Research

Researching other professionals or competitors in your field can provide valuable insights into industry trends, best practices, and areas where you can differentiate yourself. Analyze their portfolios to identify strengths, weaknesses, and opportunities for improvement. Consider the following aspects:
- **Design and User Experience:** Evaluate the visual design, layout, navigation, and usability of competitor portfolios. Identify design elements, color schemes, and typography choices that resonate with your target audience.
- **Content and Messaging:** Review the types of projects, case studies, testimonials, and client success stories featured in competitor portfolios. Identify gaps or

- or opportunities to showcase your unique skills and accomplishments.
- SEO and Online Presence: Analyze how competitors optimize their portfolios for search engines (SEO) and leverage social media platforms, professional networks, and industry forums to promote their portfolios and attract opportunities.

Setting Metrics for Success

Define key performance indicators (KPIs) to measure the effectiveness of your portfolio in achieving your goals. Track metrics such as:

- **Website Traffic:** Monitor the number of visitors, page views, and unique visitors to your portfolio over time.
- Engagement Metrics: Measure user engagement, including average session duration, bounce rate, and conversion rates (e.g., contact form submissions, project inquiries).
- **Conversion Rates:** Track the percentage of visitors who take desired actions, such as downloading your resume, subscribing to your newsletter, or scheduling a consultation.
- **Feedback and Testimonials**: Solicit feedback from peers, mentors, clients, or industry professionals to gain insights into areas for improvement and validate your portfolio's effectiveness in communicating your value proposition.

Now lets start building!

Building your Portfolio Sections

Creating a header with your name and navigation links
A well-designed header is essential for establishing your portfolio's identity and navigation. Begin by using HTML to structure your header using semantic tags like <header>, <nav>, and <ul> (unordered list) for your navigation links. Inside the <nav> element, create <a> (anchor) tags for each section of your portfolio such as "Home," "About," "Projects," "Resume," and "Contact." Use CSS to style these elements, ensuring your header is visually appealing and easy to navigate. Consider using a responsive design approach to ensure the header adjusts gracefully on different screen sizes.

Designing a hero section with a background image or video
The hero section of your portfolio is the first thing visitors see, so make it impactful and reflective of your personal brand. Use HTML to structure this section with a <section> tag and apply CSS to set a background image or video. Opt for a high-quality image or a relevant video that showcases your work or personality. Use CSS techniques such as background-size: cover; and background-position: center; to ensure the image or video fills the screen effectively. Overlay text with a contrasting color or use opacity to ensure readability.

Showcasing your projects with thumbnails, descriptions, and links
Your portfolio's project section should effectively highlight your skills and past work. Use HTML to create a grid layout using <div> tags or <ul> (unordered list)

elements for each project. Within each project container, include a thumbnail image or screenshot of the project, a brief description showcasing your role and the technologies used, and a link to view more details or the live project. Use CSS for styling, such as setting fixed dimensions for thumbnails, creating hover effects for project containers, and ensuring consistent spacing between projects.

Example Code Snippet for Project Showcase:

```html
<div class="project">
  <img src="project-thumbnail.jpg" alt="Project Thumbnail">
  <div class="project-info">
    <h3>Project Title</h3>
    <p>Description of the project and technologies used.</p>
    <a href="project-details.html" class="btn">View Project</a>
  </div>
</div>
```

Responsive Design

Responsive web design is crucial in today's digital landscape where users access websites from various devices such as smartphones, tablets, and desktops. It ensures that your portfolio looks and functions well across different screen sizes and orientations. By employing responsive design principles, you provide a seamless user experience, enhancing accessibility and engagement.

Media queries are CSS rules that enable you to apply different styles based on the characteristics of the device displaying the webpage, such as screen width, height, and orientation. Begin by targeting common device breakpoints like smartphones (320px - 767px), tablets (768px - 1023px), and desktops (1024px and above). Use media queries in your CSS to adjust layout, font sizes, margins, padding, and hide or display elements selectively based on the screen size.

Example of Media Queries:

/* Default styles for all screen sizes */

/* Tablet (768px - 1023px) */
@media screen and (min-width: 768px) and (max-width: 1023px) {
  /* Adjust styles for tablets */
}

/* Mobile (320px - 767px) */
@media screen and (max-width: 767px) {
  /* Adjust styles for smartphones */
}

/* Larger screens (1024px and above) */
@media screen and (min-width: 1024px) {
  /* Adjust styles for desktops */
}

After implementing responsive design and media queries, thoroughly test your portfolio across different devices and screen sizes. Use browser developer tools to simulate various device resolutions and orientations. Check for layout inconsistencies, text overflow, or elements that may not display correctly. Ensure that navigation remains intuitive, and all content remains accessible. Optimize images and other assets for faster loading times on mobile networks to enhance user experience further.

Media queries rely on media features, which describe the characteristics of the device being targeted. Some common media features include:

- **Width and Height:** min-width, max-width, min-height, max-height
- **Device Orientation:**
- **orientation: portrait**
- **orientation: landscape**
- **Resolution:** min-resolution and max-resolution
- **Aspect Ratio:** aspect-ratio
- **Device Type:** screen, print, speech, etc.

By combining these features with logical operators (and, not, only), developers can precisely target specific devices or conditions.

Tips for Effective Responsive Design:

- Use fluid grids and flexible units like percentages (%) for widths rather than fixed pixels (px) to allow content to adapt to different screen sizes.
- Consider using CSS frameworks like Bootstrap or Foundation that provide pre-built responsive components and grids.
- Prioritize content and ensure essential information remains accessible on smaller screens by using collapsible menus or accordion-style elements.

Finally, have fun while building!

LEVEL 4!

Color Codes Explained

Hexadecimal Color Codes Explained

Hexadecimal (base-16) color codes are alphanumeric representations of colors used in web design and digital graphics. Each color code consists of six hexadecimal digits, organized in pairs representing the intensity of red, green, and blue (RGB) components. Let's break down the basics:

Counting in Hexadecimal

Hexadecimal numbers use digits 0-9 and letters A-F to represent values. This system is based on powers of 16, where each digit's position signifies a power of 16, starting from 16^0 (units place) to 16^5 (highest place). For example:

- 0x346:
- $3×16^2$ (16 to the second power) (3 times 256 = 768)
- $4×16^4$ (16 to the fourth power)(4 times 16 = 64)
- $6×16^0$ (16 to the power of 0) (6 times 1 = 6)
- Total: 838 in base-10

Additive Color Theory

Additive color mixing is used in digital displays where colors are created by combining different intensities of red, green, and blue light (RGB). Key concepts include:

- RGB Components: Each hexadecimal pair in a color code represents the intensity of red, green, and blue:
    - #RRGGBB
    - Example: #FF0000 (full red, no green or blue)
- Color Mixing: Unlike subtractive color mixing (as in print), where colors mix to form darker hues, additive mixing results in lighter colors:
    - Red + Green = Yellow (#FFFF00)
    - Red + Blue = Magenta
    - Green + Blue = Cyan
    - Red + Green + Blue = White (#FFFFFF)
    - Absence of all colors = Black (#000000)

Practical Examples

- #FF0000 vs #330000:
    - #FF0000 is bright red (full red, no green or blue)
    - #330000 has less red than #FF0000, resulting in a darker shade of red.
- #FFFFFF and #000000:
    - #FFFFFF is pure white (maximum intensity of all RGB components).
    - #000000 is pure black (absence of all RGB components).

Applying Color Codes in Design

Understanding hexadecimal color codes allows designers to:

- Consistently Use Colors: Ensure colors remain consistent across digital platforms.
- Achieve Desired Visual Effects: Control color intensity

- and combinations for optimal visual impact.
- Enhance User Experience: Create accessible designs with sufficient color contrast.

Draw and practice your design beforehand.

LEVEL 5!

Javascript

What is JavaScript?

JavaScript is a powerful and versatile programming language used to create dynamic and interactive experiences on websites. Whether you're building a simple webpage or a full-scale web application, JavaScript is the tool that makes it all come to life. It's one of the core technologies of the web, alongside HTML (for structure) and CSS (for styling). When you visit a webpage that includes interactive elements like forms, animations, pop-up messages, or auto-updating content, it's JavaScript running behind the scenes. It turns static webpages into dynamic ones that can respond to user input and perform actions in real-time.

Why is JavaScript Essential for Web Development?

JavaScript is essential for creating engaging user experiences on the web. It allows developers to:

- Add interactivity to websites (e.g., buttons, forms).
- Create animations and transitions.
- Handle real-time updates without reloading the entire page (AJAX).
- Develop complex web applications like email clients, social networks, or interactive maps.

JavaScript is supported by all modern web browsers, which means that learning it opens up endless possibilities for building web applications and interactive sites.
Types of Applications You Can Build with JavaScript
JavaScript is highly versatile and can be used to build:
- Websites: From static content to dynamic, interactive web pages.
- Web Applications: Tools like email clients, messaging apps, or project management tools.
- Games: JavaScript can be used to develop browser-based games.
- Mobile Apps: Using frameworks like React Native or Ionic, developers can build mobile apps with JavaScript.
- Server-Side Applications: With Node.js, JavaScript can also be used to write server-side logic, making it possible to handle databases, user authentication, and more.

Setting Up JavaScript in a Web Page

To get started with JavaScript, you need to include it in your HTML file. This is typically done by linking to an external JavaScript file or by writing JavaScript directly within the HTML file using the <script> tag.

Let's begin with a simple example. First, create an HTML file called index.html. This file will be your webpage:

```html
<!DOCTYPE html>
<html lang="en">
<head>
    <meta charset="UTF-8">
    <meta name="viewport" content="width=device-width, initial-scale=1.0">
    <title>My First JavaScript Page</title>
</head>
<body>
    <h1>Hello, World!</h1>
    <p>This is my first JavaScript example.</p>

    <!-- Link to external JavaScript file -->
    <script src="main.js"></script>
</body>
</html>
```

In this HTML file, we have a script tag that links to a file called main.js. This file will contain our JavaScript code. Next, create a file called main.js in the same directory as your HTML file. Inside main.js, write the following:

```javascript
const myHeading = document.querySelector("h1");
    myHeading.textContent = "Hello world!";
```

The heading text was changed to Hello world! using JavaScript. You accomplished this by calling querySelector() to obtain a reference to your heading and storing it in a variable called myHeading. This is identical to what we accomplished with CSS selectors. When you wish to make changes to an element, you must first select it.

Quick Run Through of Javascript

Variables
- Variables are used to store data.

Use let for variables you plan to reassign, and const for ones that won't change.

Ex.
let name = "Alice";
const age = 25;

Data Types
JavaScript has several data types, including:
- String: Text inside quotes ("Hello").
- Number: Numeric values (42).
- Boolean: true or false.
- Array: List of values ([1, 2, 3]).
- Object: Key-value pairs ({name: "Alice", age: 25}).

Basic Operators
You can use operators to perform calculations and compare values.
- Arithmetic Operators: +, -, *, /
- Comparison Operators: ==, ===, !=, !==, >, <

Example:
let x = 10;
let y = 5;
let result = x + y; // 15

Control Structures

59

Conditional Statements:

```
if (x > 5) { console.log("x is greater than 5"); } else
{ console.log("x is 5 or less"); }
```

Loops let you repeat actions:

```
for (let i = 0; i < 5; i++) {
  console.log(i);
}
```

while loop

```
let i = 0;
while (i < 5) {
 console.log(i);
 i++;
}
```

Functions

Functions are blocks of code that perform tasks. You can define and call functions to reuse code.

```
function greet(name) { return "Hello, " + name; }
console.log(greet("Alice")); // Hello, Alice
```

Array

Arrays are collections of values that can be accessed by index.

```
let fruits = ["apple", "banana", "cherry"];
console.log(fruits[0]); // apple
```

How JavaScript is Used in Building Websites

JavaScript plays a crucial role in building interactive, dynamic, and functional websites. Here's a breakdown of how JavaScript is used in web development:

Making Web Pages Interactive

While HTML provides the structure of a web page and CSS styles its appearance, JavaScript adds life to your website by allowing users to interact with the page. For example:

- Handling User Input: JavaScript can react to user actions like clicks, keyboard inputs, or form submissions.
- Displaying Alerts or Popups: You can trigger popups or alerts based on certain conditions.
- Updating Content Dynamically: You can change the text, images, or other content on a web page without reloading the entire page.

example:
**document.querySelector("button").addEventListener("click", function() {
document.querySelector("p").textContent = "Button clicked!"; });**

Manipulating the DOM (Document Object Model)

JavaScript can directly interact with HTML elements using the DOM. The DOM represents the HTML structure of your web page, and JavaScript can manipulate it in real-time.

- Selecting Elements: JavaScript can select HTML elements to modify them.
- Changing Styles: JavaScript can change CSS styles directly.
- Adding/Removing Elements: You can create, remove, or alter elements dynamically.

document.body.style.backgroundColor = "lightblue";

Form Validation

JavaScript is often used to validate forms before they are submitted, ensuring that users provide correct and complete information.

example:
```
let form = document.querySelector("form"); form.addEventListener("submit", function(event) { let name = document.querySelector("#name").value; if (name === "") { alert("Name is required!"); event.preventDefault(); // Stop form submission } });
```

Creating Dynamic User Interfaces

JavaScript can create rich, interactive UIs without needing to reload the web page. Common uses include:
- Carousels: Rotating image galleries.
- Tabs and Accordion Menus: Organizing content in compact areas.
- Animations: Smooth transitions, movements, or effects on elements.

Overall, JavaScript is required for creating modern websites. It improves the engagement and interactivity of web pages, validates user input, and allows for the dynamic loading or updating of material without requiring a full reload. Whether you're improving forms, modifying page elements, or designing sophisticated user interfaces, JavaScript has the tools you need to create a dynamic and responsive web experience.

Future Learning

Website Ideas

Tribute Pages

- A tribute page is a simple yet meaningful project that pays homage to a person, group, or concept. It typically includes:
- Design Elements: Incorporating images, typography, and colors that reflect the theme of the tribute.
- Content Structure: Presenting biographical information, achievements, and significant milestones.
- Interactive Features: Optional interactive elements such as image sliders or timelines to enhance user engagement.

Webpage with User Input

- Creating a webpage with user input involves building forms or interactive elements where users can contribute content, provide feedback, or interact with data. Key considerations include:
- Form Design: Designing intuitive and accessible forms using HTML and CSS.
- Validation: Implementing client-side and server-side

validation to ensure data integrity and security.
- Data Handling: Storing user input in databases or utilizing APIs to process and display user-generated content dynamically.

Fake Restaurant Page

Designing a mock-up restaurant page allows for creative exploration of:
- Menu Design: Creating visually appealing menus with pricing, descriptions, and images.
- Reservation System: Implementing a reservation form with date/time selection and confirmation.
- Location and Contact Information: Integrating Google Maps for location visualization and contact details for customer inquiries.

Music Store Page

A music store page can showcase:
- Product Catalog: Displaying albums, tracks, merchandise with descriptions, prices, and cover art.
- Shopping Cart: Implementing a cart system for users to add items and proceed to checkout.
- Audio Integration: Integrating audio previews or streaming services for music listening.

Photography Site

A photography website focuses on visual storytelling and portfolio display:
- Gallery Display: Showcasing photography portfolios with categorized albums or projects.
- Image Optimization: Implementing techniques for image loading optimization to maintain visual quality and performance.
- Client Interaction: Including features like client galleries, contact forms for inquiries, and booking requests.

Personal Portfolio (You've Done This!)
- A personal portfolio serves as a showcase of your skills, projects, and achievements:
- Design: Crafting a visually appealing and user-friendly interface that reflects your personal brand.
- Project Showcase: Highlighting key projects with descriptions, images, and links to detailed case studies.
- Contact and About Sections: Providing information about yourself, your skills, and ways to get in touch.

Blog
- Creating a blog involves establishing a platform for sharing insights, experiences, and knowledge:
- Content Management: Implementing a content management system (CMS) like WordPress or developing a custom solution.
- Categories and Tags: Organizing posts by categories and tags for easy navigation and content discovery.
- Comments and Interaction: Enabling user comments, social sharing buttons, and email subscriptions for reader engagement.

Domains to Publish

Web hosting services provide the infrastructure and technologies needed for a website to be accessible via the Internet. Key components of hosting services include:

- Server Types: Shared hosting, VPS (Virtual Private Server), dedicated servers, and cloud hosting, each offering different levels of performance and scalability.
- Uptime and Reliability: Ensuring your website remains operational with minimal downtime is essential for maintaining user trust and SEO rankings.

Consider these established hosting providers known for their reliability, customer support, and range of services:

1. Bluehost: Known for its user-friendly interface and affordable hosting plans, suitable for beginners and small businesses. Offers WordPress hosting and domain registration services.
2. SiteGround: Renowned for excellent customer support, fast loading times, and robust security features. Offers shared hosting, cloud hosting, and managed WordPress hosting.
3. HostGator: Provides a wide range of hosting options including shared, VPS, and dedicated hosting. Known for its scalability and user-friendly control panel.
4. DreamHost: Offers reliable hosting with unlimited bandwidth and storage options. Known for its commitment to privacy and strong customer support.
5. GoDaddy: One of the largest domain registrars, offering a variety of hosting plans including shared hosting, VPS hosting, and managed WordPress hosting. Also provides domain registration services.

Factors to Consider

When evaluating hosting providers, consider these factors to ensure they meet your needs:

- Performance: Check for uptime guarantees and server response times to ensure fast loading speeds for your website visitors.
- Scalability: Assess whether the hosting provider can accommodate your website's growth in terms of traffic and resource demands.
- Security: Look for SSL certificates, regular backups, and robust security measures to protect your website and user data.
- Support: Evaluate the quality and availability of customer support, including options for live chat, .

phone support, and knowledge base resources.

Choosing the Right Plan
- Select a hosting plan based on your specific requirements:
- Shared Hosting: Affordable for small websites with moderate traffic.
- VPS Hosting: Offers more resources and flexibility than shared hosting.
- Dedicated Hosting: Provides maximum control and performance for high-traffic websites or applications.
- Managed WordPress Hosting: Optimized for WordPress websites with automatic updates and enhanced security features

Future Books

Here's a sneak peek at the exciting lineup of upcoming books designed to cater to absolute beginners across various programming languages and concepts:

1. Simple, Quick, Python Coding
- 10 Coding Activities: Hands-on exercises to reinforce learning and practical application.
- Clear Explanations: Step-by-step guidance on Python basics, syntax, and core concepts.
- Practical Examples: Real-world scenarios to help apply Python skills effectively.

2. Flowcharts and Pseudocode: Understand How They Work for Absolute Beginners
- Concept Clarity: Simplified explanations of flowchart symbols and pseudocode structures.
- Practical Exercises: Practice problems to reinforce understanding and problem-solving skills.

- Application Scenarios: Insight into how flowcharts and pseudocode are used in programming and problem-solving contexts.

3. Caffeinated, Versatile Java for Absolute Beginners
- Visual Learning Approach: Illustrations, diagrams, and visual aids to enhance comprehension.
- 10 Coding Activities: Interactive coding exercises to reinforce Java programming skills.
- Comprehensive Coverage: From basic syntax to object-oriented programming concepts in Java.

Way 2 Eazy

Way2Eazy offers **free** courses and classes about computer science or math. To book a **free** tutoring class, use the contact form on the bottom of the website. All classes and courses are **free**.

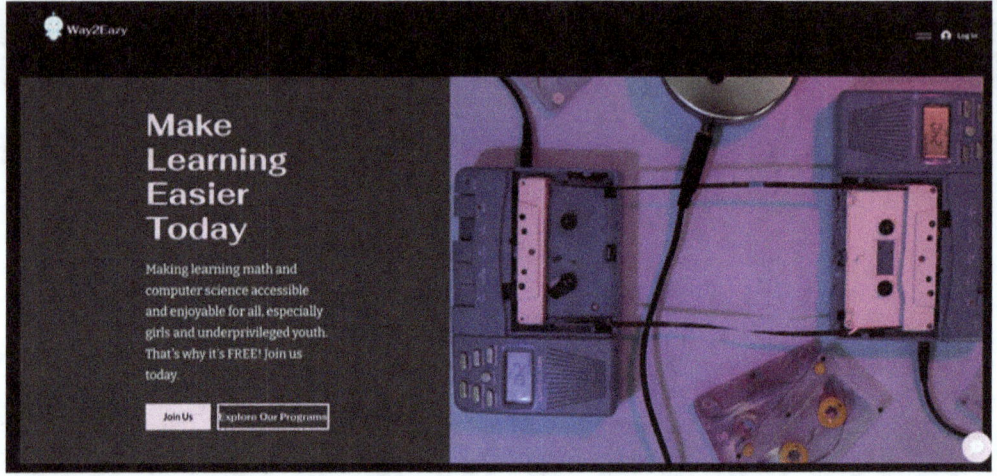

You can learn Java and more HTML and CSS all from the comfort of your home! We also host beginner-friendly hackathons for those wanting to try a mini one before a major one. Join Us today.

for any questions, visit **way2eazy.org** for more help! This book is supposed to be enjoyable, easy to read, and helpful, so enjoy coding!

LEVEL 7!

Take Notes

Majella Rajan is a highschool student, intrigued by technology. Recognized by the **National Center for Women in Technology (NCWIT)** as an Aspirations in Computing Regional winner, she works to close the gender disparity within the field of computer science and engineering by teaching students while taking her own interest in studies.

visit her website majellarajan.com

Yay! You learned how to build a website using HTML and CSS and a tiny bit of Javascript!! Now as you go forward in your coding journey, you can reminisce on the times you began coding through notes and activites.

www.ingramcontent.com/pod-product-compliance
Lightning Source LLC
Chambersburg PA
CBHW062315220526
45479CB00004B/1177